Developing Numeracy

NUMBERS AND THE NUMBER SYSTEM

ACTIVITIES FOR THE DAILY MATHS LESSON

COUNTING AND RECOGNISING NUMBERS

year

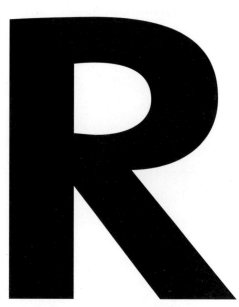

R

Paul Broadbent

A & C BLACK

D0537942

Contents

Comparing and ordering numbers

Resource sheets

Published 1999 by A&C Black (Publishers) Limited
35 Bedford Row, London WC1R 4JH

ISBN O-7136-5237-3

Copyright text © Paul Broadbent, 1999
Copyright illustrations © Martin Pierce, 1999
Copyright cover illustration © Charlotte Hard, 1999

The authors and publisher would like to thank the following teachers for their advice in producing this series of books:
Tracy Adam; Shilpa Bharambe; Hardip Channa; Sue Hall; Ann Hart; Lydia Hunt; Madeleine Madden; Helen Mason;
Anne Norbury; Jane Siddons; Judith Wells; Fleur Whatley.

A CIP catalogue record for this book is available from the British Library.

All rights reserved. This book may be photocopied, for use in the school or educational establishment for which it was purchased,
but may not be reproduced in any other form or by any means – graphic, electronic or mechanical, including recording, taping
or information retrieval systems – without the prior permission in writing of the publishers.

Printed in Great Britain by St Edmundsbury Press Ltd, Bury St Edmunds, Suffolk.

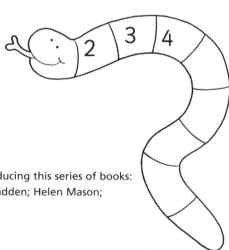

Introduction

Developing Numeracy: Numbers and the Number System is a series of seven photocopiable activity books designed to be used during the daily maths lesson. They focus on the first strand of the National Numeracy Strategy *Framework for teaching mathematics*. The activities are intended to be used in the time allocated to pupil activities; they aim to reinforce the teaching within the lesson and provide practice and consolidation of the objectives contained in the framework document.

Year R supports the teaching of mathematics to reception age children by providing a series of activities that develop essential skills in counting and recognising numbers. All the activities are designed to enable children to work independently, with clearly written instructions to guide them. However, it is expected that some teacher support will be needed.

Year R:

- introduces and focuses on the numbers zero to ten, developing the sense of the size of a number and the counting system;
- includes activities which focus on the reading, writing, comparing and ordering of numbers;
- promotes independent work during the daily maths lesson with low guidance activities;
- encourages the use of the correct mathematical language.

Extension

Many of the activity sheets end with a challenge (**Now try this!**) which reinforces and extends the children's learning, and provides the teacher with the opportunity for assessment. Due to the age of the children, the teacher may wish to read out the instructions and explain the activity before they begin working on it.

Organisation

The activities require very few additional resources but it will be useful to have available coloured pencils, interlocking cubes, dice, counters, scissors and glue. Several of the sheets involve cutting out and sticking, which can be done by the children or adults as appropriate. Several activities can be re-used if the appropriate areas of the pages are masked before copying and different numbers substituted to provide variety or differentiation. It may often be helpful to provide the children with number lines to help them to complete the activities. Photocopiable resource sheets (including a certificate to recognise individual children's achievements) are provided at the end of the book.

To help teachers to select appropriate learning experiences for their children, the activities are grouped into sections within each book. The pages are not intended to be presented in the order in which they appear unless otherwise stated.

Structure of the daily maths lesson

The recommended structure of the daily maths lesson for Key Stage 1 is as follows:

Start to lesson, oral work, mental calculation	5-10 minutes
Main teaching and pupil activities	about 30 minutes
Plenary	about 10 minutes

A reception class may be organised slightly differently, as follows:

- an introduction with the whole class which may include finger games, number rhymes and songs;
- some teaching of the whole class on the main maths topic for the day;
- group activities – either all the children divided into small groups working simultaneously on the same area of maths, or groups of children taking part in turn throughout the day in one or more play activities linked to the theme of the lesson, usually supported by an adult. The activities in the **Developing Numeracy** series are designed to be carried out during the time allocated to group activities;
- a plenary with the whole class after the group activities are ended to consolidate and extend the children's learning through questions and discussion.

The following chart shows an example of the way in which an activity from this book can be used to achieve the required organisation of the daily maths lesson for reception age children.

Five little speckled frogs (page 37)

Start to the lesson	
As a whole class introduction to the lesson, sing the number song 'Five little speckled frogs' with the children. Once all the children are familiar with the song, a group of children could be chosen to come to the front of the class and perform the actions while the song is sung again. Point out to the children that in singing the song they have been counting backwards from five to zero.	**5-10 minutes**

Group activities	
The children then work on a variety of activities. One group could practise counting a set of five pencils (for example), and then each child could be given a set of fewer pencils and challenged to say how many more they will need to have five. Another group of children could collect a variety of objects (e.g. rulers, beads, building bricks) and sort them into groups, counting the number of objects in each group. The other children could work, with minimal intervention, from **Five little speckled frogs** (page 37, **Developing Numeracy: Numbers and the Number System Year R**).	**about 30 minutes**

Plenary	
During the plenary session, the children could talk about how they count on and back from zero to five and the song could be sung again.	**about 10 minutes**

Teachers' notes

Very brief notes are provided at the bottom of most pages, giving ideas and suggestions for maximising the effectiveness of the activity sheets. These notes could be masked before photocopying.

Further activities

The following activities provide some practical ideas for teaching children how to count and recognise numbers. They are intended to introduce or reinforce the main teaching part of the lesson.

Reading and writing numbers

Behind the wall
Once the children have completed the activities on pages 11 to 21, which introduce the numbers zero to ten, their learning can be reinforced by playing 'Behind the wall'. Slide a number card up from behind a 'wall' (which could be any suitable screen such as a piece of card or a book). Slide the number up slowly so that it just peeps over the top of the 'wall' and ask which number it might be. Keep showing a little more of the number until the children work out which number it is. Repeat for other numbers.

Show me
Each child has a set of numeral cards 0 to 9 (see page 62). Play 'show me' activities where each child shows a number card by holding it up in the air as you say, "Show me the number 5", "show me the number 3", "show me 0", etc. Hold up a numeral card yourself and ask the children to show a number like it; what does it say? Numeral cards to 20 (see page 63) may be used in the same way when children are ready to explore numbers to ten and beyond.

Numbers all around us
Talk to the children about where they can see numbers in the environment, around the home and in the street as well as in parks, public buildings, shops and restaurants (for example, on front doors, telephones, road signs, petrol pumps, cars, televisions, microwaves, clocks, price tags and menus).

All about the number...
The children could make a scrapbook or poster of numerals cut from magazines, catalogues and birthday cards, with each number having a page of its own. They could draw pictures to illustrate the numbers.

Making numbers
The children could use plasticine, sand, corrugated paper or sandpaper to make the different numerals. They could close their eyes and try to guess which number has been put in their hand.

Numbers in the air
On large pieces of paper, use one colour to write a number, such as 1, that is written in a continuous stroke, and two colours to write the numbers that need two strokes, such as 4 and 5 (writing the first stroke in one colour and the second in another). Ask individual children to stand and point to each number, tracing the separate strokes in the air. This will help the children to see the different strokes needed when writing numerals. Discuss the variations in number formation between left- and right-handed children.

Counting

Action rhymes
There are many action rhymes that can help to build children's confidence and pleasure in counting as they sing, chant or join in with the actions. These include 'Five little speckled frogs' (see page 37), 'One, two, three, four, five, Once I caught a fish alive' (see page 42), 'The beehive', 'Ten little mice', 'Five fat sausages', One, two, buckle my shoe' and 'On the first day of Christmas'.

Count in turn
Children stand in a line facing the same direction. They stamp gently as they count and throw their arms up in the air for the last number in the counting sequence. As the last number is said, they turn and begin the counting sequence again, keeping to a regular rhythm. They could also clap in time to the count. If there are more than ten children in a line, the eleventh child could either begin the sequence again, or perhaps begin to count beyond ten.

Boston wave
Children sit in a circle and count slowly in unison, "*one, two, three, four, five; one, two, three, four, five,*" and so on. Decide in which direction the Boston wave will go; then, as *one* is chanted, point to a child who quickly stands up and sits down. Point to the next child as *two* is chanted, who again has quickly to stand up and sit down. Continue around the circle. With practice, there will be no need to point; children will automatically continue the Boston wave around the circle.

Thigh, clap, snap, snap
Sit in a circle and slowly slap the tops of your legs, then clap hands and snap fingers, first with one hand and then with the other, developing a steady rhythm. Count each number from one to four in time to the actions:

thigh	clap	snap	snap	thigh	clap	snap	snap
1	2	3	4	1	2	3	4

These counting activities can be developed to give practice in counting backwards and forwards (see pages 48-51), counting in tens (see page 52) and counting in twos (see pages 53-54).

Comparing and ordering numbers

People numbers
Give out one set of large numeral cards from 0 to 10. The children holding the numeral cards stand facing the rest of the class. Ask them to arrange themselves in order, from 0 to 10. Ask individual children who are not holding a number to change places with a numeral chosen by you. ("*Sam change places with the number three; Emma change places with the number eight.*") Use the language of position, such as before and after, within this. ("*Ali change places with any number before the number three.*")

Washing lines
String up a washing line in part of the classroom and give children numbers to hang on the washing line using small bulldog clips. Ask the children to hang the numbers in order. When all the numbers are in position, ask the children to identify particular numbers. ("*Point to the number six*"; "*point to the number between two and four*"; "*point to the number before five.*") In all these activities, use the language of comparison (such as more or less, greater or smaller) and the language of order (first, last, before, after, next, between).

Show me
Children could hold up numeral cards to show the answers to instructions such as "*Show me a number... greater than 3... smaller than 8... between 6 and 9,*" and "*Show me... 1 more than 7... 1 less than 4*".

Number rods
Use number rods such as multilink or cuisenaire rods. Talk about comparing and ordering the rods and then ask the children to arrange a group of rods in size order.

Line patterns

- ## Trace over the lines.

- ## Continue the lines.

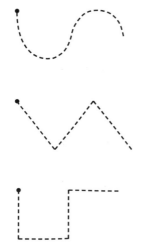

Teachers' note Encourage the children to develop their dexterity in forming these shapes by making the line patterns in trays of sand, repeating each pattern until the size is consistent.

Developing Numeracy
Numbers and the Number System
Year R
© A & C Black 1999

Number snakes 0 to 3

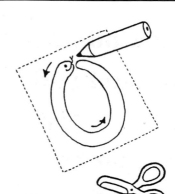

- **Trace the number snakes.**
- **Start at the head.**
- **Finish at the tail.**
- **Say the number.**

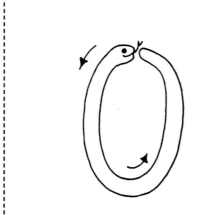

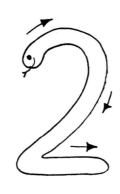

- **Cut out the number snakes.**
- **Make a number strip.**

0	1	2	3

Teachers' note Encourage the children to practise writing numbers in the air, starting at the top of the number. To make the number strip, provide for each child a strip of paper, 9-10 cm wide and 100 cm long, on to which the children can glue the numbers from pages 8-10 in the correct order. These number strips can be coloured and displayed.

Developing Numeracy
Numbers and the Number System
Year R
© A & C Black 1999

Number snakes 4 to 7

- **Trace the number snakes.**
- **Start at the head.**
- **Finish at the tail.**
- **Say the number.**

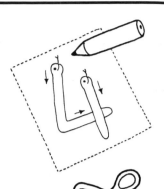

- **Cut out the number snakes.**
- **Make a number strip.**

4	5	6	7

Teachers' note Children may have problems forming the numbers four and five because of the two strokes. Encourage them to practise the first stroke of each number until it is mastered before going on to the second stroke. For left-handed children, adjustments may need to be made to the directional arrows.

Developing Numeracy
Numbers and the Number System
Year R
© A & C Black 1999

Number snakes 8 to 10

- **Trace the number snakes.**
- **Start at the head.**
- **Finish at the tail.**
- **Say the number.**

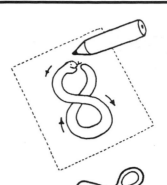

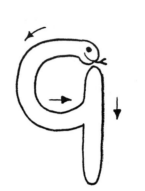

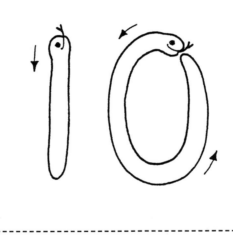

- **Cut out the number snakes.**
- **Make a number strip.**

8	9	10

Teachers' note Left-handed children may write the number eight in the opposite direction to right-handed children, so adjustments may need to be made to the directional arrows. Remind the children that the number nine is formed in a continuous stroke; the pencil should not be lifted from the paper.

Developing Numeracy
Numbers and the Number System
Year R
© A & C Black 1999

All about 0

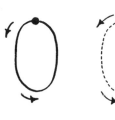 

- **Trace over the numbers.**
- **Start on the dot.**

There are **0** people at the bus stop.

- **Draw a house with no door.**
- **Draw no chimneys on the roof.**

- **Colour the bicycles with no wheels.**

Teachers' note Zero is an important concept for children to understand. Introduce the idea of the empty set. Practise counting backwards from five to zero.

Developing Numeracy
Numbers and the Number System
Year R
© A & C Black 1999

All about I

- **Trace the over the numbers.**
- **Start on the dot.**

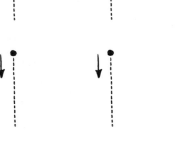

There is **I** person at the bus stop.

- **Draw I flower.**
- **Draw I bee on the flower.**

- **Colour the leaves with I caterpillar.**

Now try this!

Teachers' note The children could point to examples of single objects around the classroom.

Developing Numeracy
Numbers and the Number System
Year R
© A & C Black 1999

- **Trace over the numbers.**
- **Start on the dot.**

There are **2** people at the bus stop.

- **Draw 2 eyes on the dog.**
- **Draw 2 ears on the cat.**

- **Colour the things with 2 legs.**

Now try this!

Teachers' note The children could make a scrapbook with a page for every number. They could draw pictures of objects to match that number, for example, two cars on the page for number 2.

**Developing Numeracy
Numbers and the Number System
Year R**
© A & C Black 1999

All about 3

Developing Numeracy
Numbers and the Number System
Year R
© A & C Black 1999

- Trace over the numbers.
- Start on the dot.

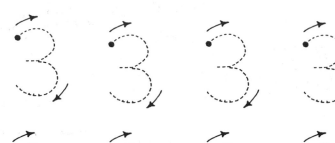

There are **3** people at the bus stop.

- Draw 3 sausages on the plate.
- Draw 3 eggs on the plate.

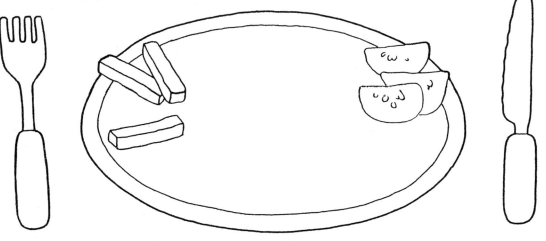

- Colour the plates with 3 cakes.

Now try this!

14

All about 4

• **Trace over the numbers.**

• **Start on the dots.**

There are **4** people at the bus stop.

• **Draw 4 windows on the house.**

• **Draw 4 people in the garden.**

• **Colour the flowers with 4 petals.**

Now try this!

Teachers' note Use cubes or counters to develop this activity, by looking at arrangements that make four, for example, one and three; two and two.

Developing Numeracy
Numbers and the Number System
Year R
© A & C Black 1999

All about 5

- **Trace over the numbers.**
- **Start on the dots.**

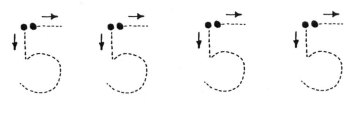

There are **5** people at the bus stop.

- **Draw 5 balloons.**

- **Colour the cakes with 5 candles.**

Now try this!

Teachers' note Use cubes or counters to develop this activity by looking at arrangements that make five, for example, one and four; two and three. For left-handed children, adjustments may need to be made to the directional arrows.

Developing Numeracy
Numbers and the Number System
Year R
© A & C Black 1999

16

All about 6

- **Trace over the numbers.**
- **Start on the dot.**

> There are **6** people at the bus stop.

- **Draw 6 rocks in the sea.**
- **Draw 6 bits of seaweed.**

- **Colour the fish with 6 bubbles.**

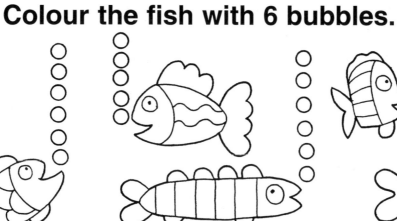

Teachers' note Use cubes or counters to develop this activity by looking at arrangements that make six, for example, three and three; four and two.

Developing Numeracy
Numbers and the Number System
Year R
© A & C Black 1999

17

All about 7

There are **7** people at the bus stop.

- **Trace over the numbers.**
- **Start on the dot.**

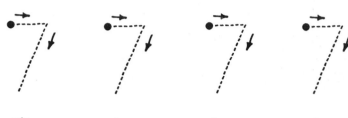

- **Draw 7 eggs in the nest.**
- **Draw 7 leaves on the tree.**

Now try this!

- **Colour the nests with 7 birds.**

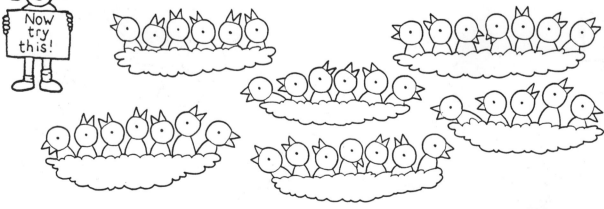

Developing Numeracy
Numbers and the Number System
Year R
© A & C Black 1999

All about 8

There are **8** people at the bus stop.

- **Trace over the numbers.**
- **Start on the dot.**

- **Draw 8 bananas in the bowl.**
- **Draw 8 oranges in the bowl.**

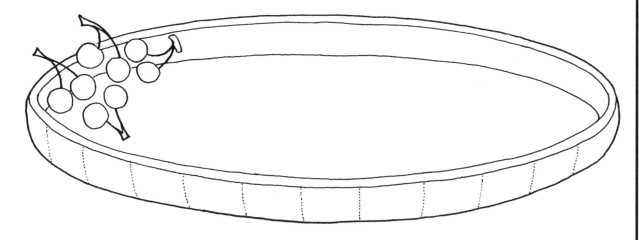

- **Colour the bunches of 8 grapes.**

Now try this!

Teachers' note Left-handed children may write the number eight in the opposite direction to right-handed children, so adjustments may need to be made to the directional arrows.

Developing Numeracy
Numbers and the Number System
Year R
© A & C Black 1999

All about 9

- **Trace over the numbers.**
- **Start on the dot.**

There are **9** people at the bus stop.

- **Draw 9 apples in the basket.**
- **Draw 9 cherries on the tree.**

- **Colour the trees with 9 pears.**

Now try this!

Teachers' note Remind the children that the number nine is formed in a continuous stroke; the pencil should not be lifted from the paper.

Developing Numeracy
Numbers and the Number System
Year R
© A & C Black 1999

All about 10

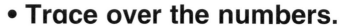

- **Trace over the numbers.**
- **Start on the dots.**

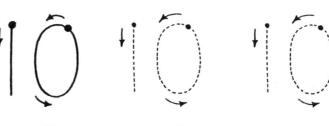

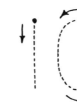

There are **10** people at the bus stop.

- **Draw 10 spots on the umbrella.**
- **Draw 10 puddles on the ground.**

- **Colour the clouds with 10 raindrops.**

Now try this!

Developing Numeracy
Numbers and the Number System
Year R
© A & C Black 1999

21

- **Trace the number snakes.**
- **Start on the dot.**
- **Say the number.**

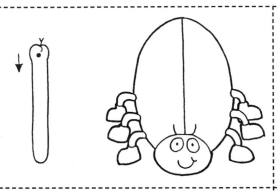

- **Draw spots on each ladybird to match the number.**
- **Cut out the cards.**
- **Put them in order.**

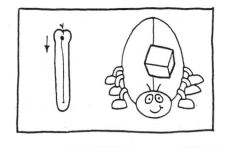

| 1 | 2 | 3 | 4 | 5 |

Now try this!

- **Place cubes on each card to match the number.**

Teachers' note Use the cards to ask 'show me' questions, for example, "Show me the number three"; "show me two more than three"; "show me the number between one and three".

Developing Numeracy
Numbers and the Number System
Year R
© A & C Black 1999

Match the spots 2

- **Trace the number snakes.**
- **Start on the dot.**
- **Say the number.**

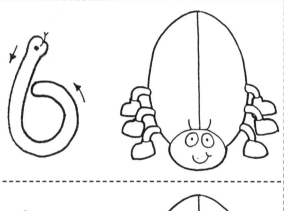  

- **Draw spots on each ladybird to match the number.**

- **Cut out the cards.**
- **Put them in order.**

| 6 | 7 | 8 | 9 | 10 |

- **Place cubes on each card to match the number.**

Teachers' note Use the cards to ask 'show me' questions, for example, "Show me the number seven"; "show me one more than eight"; "show me a number smaller than eight".

**Developing Numeracy
Numbers and the Number System
Year R**
© A & C Black 1999

Numbers at sea

- **Write the numbers inside the outlines.**

- **Cut out the cards.**

- **Mix them up.**

- **Match each number card to a picture card.**

Teachers' note The children could also use these cards (or multiple sets of them) to play number and picture 'snap'.

Developing Numeracy
Numbers and the Number System
Year R
© A & C Black 1999

Rainy day numbers

- **Join each set of objects to a number.**

- **Write each of these numbers in a cloud.**

| 1 | 2 | 3 | 4 | 5 |

- **Draw raindrops below each cloud to match the number.**

Teachers' note As an extension activity, ask the children to draw five more clouds on a piece of paper. Ask them to write any other numbers to 20 in the clouds and then draw snowflakes or raindrops below the clouds to match the numbers.

Developing Numeracy
Numbers and the Number System
Year R
© A & C Black 1999

- **Count the things in the pictures.**
- **Trace the numbers.**
- **Draw a new set of things to match the number.**

Teachers' note If the children find it difficult to draw in the spaces, they could stick small stickers in the boxes to show the numbers. When the children have completed the activity, you could ask them to count the total number of objects in each row and point out to them that the number is double the starting number for that row.

Developing Numeracy
Numbers and the Number System
Year R
© A & C Black 1999

In the sweet shop

• **Write the price on each label.**

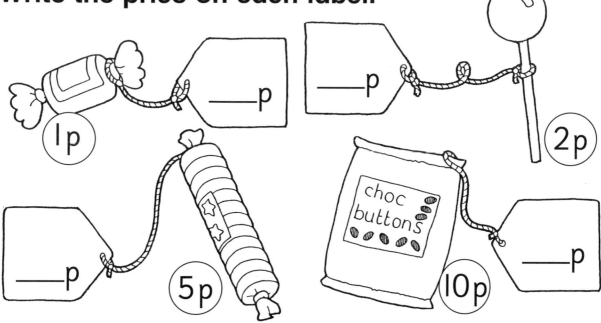

• **Make up a price for each of these things.**

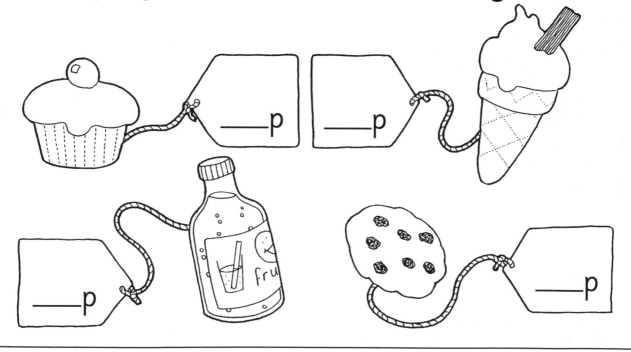

• **With a partner, take turns to choose something in the picture.**
• **Pay the correct number of pennies for it.**

Teachers' note The labels on the page could be cut out, or the children could make their own labels and write prices on them for items in a class shop. Provide the children with 1p, 2p and 5p coins and encourage them to play shops.

Developing Numeracy
Numbers and the Number System
Year R
© A & C Black 1999

Matching game: numbers

- **Cut out the number cards.**
- **Say the number on each card.**
- **Write the number in the circle.**

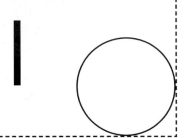

1 ◯	6 ◯
2 ◯	7 ◯
3 ◯	8 ◯
4 ◯	9 ◯
5 ◯	10 ◯

Teachers' note After the activity the children should cut out the picture cards on page 29 and match them to the number cards. Make sure that the children understand that the last number in the count gives that set its number name.

Developing Numeracy
Numbers and the Number System
Year R
© A & C Black 1999

Matching game: pictures

- ● **Cut out the picture cards.**
- ● **Count the objects in each picture.**
- ● **Match each picture to a number card.**

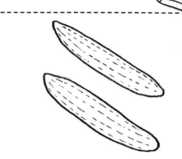

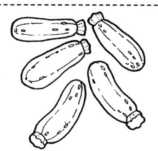

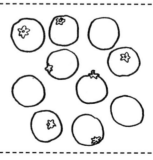

Teachers' note When the children are counting the objects in each picture, observe the methods they use, such as just looking and counting; touching the objects and counting; or counting the objects in groups.

**Developing Numeracy
Numbers and the Number System
Year R**
© A & C Black 1999

The toy shop

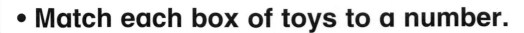

- **Match each box of toys to a number.**

0
1
2
3
4
5

Now try this!

- **Write the correct number in each box.**

- **Colour the picture.**

The clown has:

 ☐ red nose

 ☐ green fingers

○ ○ ☐ blue eyes

☐ yellow buttons

Developing Numeracy
Numbers and the Number System
Year R
© A & C Black 1999

Jewellery box

- **Count the jewels in each ring.**

- **Match each ring to a number word.**

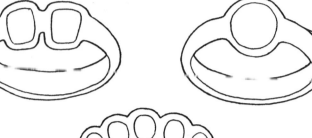

one
two
three
four
five

- **Trace the numbers and the words on the number necklaces.**

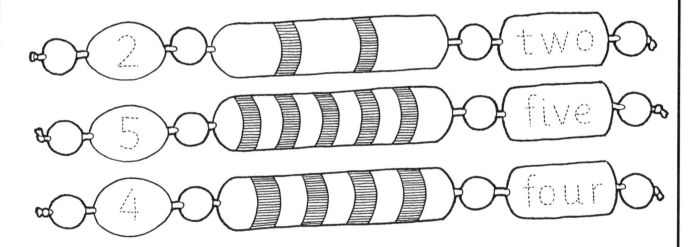

- **Draw a number necklace for** `one` **.**

- **Draw a number necklace for** `three` **.**

Developing Numeracy
Numbers and the Number System
Year R
© A & C Black 1999

31

Number dominoes

• **Draw dots on each domino to match the number.**

zero	

three	

one	

four	

two	

five	

• **Write the correct number on each domino.**

zero	

three	

one	

four	

two	

five	

Teachers' note Teach the children how to play dominoes with a complete set, counting and matching the dots.

**Developing Numeracy
Numbers and the Number System
Year R**
© A & C Black 1999

Dice game

- **Roll a dice 10 times.**
- **Put a mark on the chart for each number you roll.**

one	1 ⚀	
two	2 ⚁	
three	3 ⚂	
four	4 ⚃	
five	5 ⚄	
six	6 ⚅	

Now try this!

- **Roll the dice.**
- **Colour the number name.**
- **Continue until every number is coloured.**

five   one   three   four   two   six

Teachers' note Show the children how to keep a tally, making single marks or groups of five.

Developing Numeracy
Numbers and the Number System
Year R
© A & C Black 1999

Snap: number cards

- **Cut out the cards.**
- **Match each number card to a word card.**

2	6	9	3	8
4	10	1	7	5
five	one	seven	three	ten
four	nine	eight	six	two

- **Put the pairs of cards in order.**

Start with | 1 | one |

Teachers' note Use the cards on this page with those on page 35. As a further extension, the children could play 'snap' or 'pairs' with two of the three sets of number, word and picture cards.

**Developing Numeracy
Numbers and the Number System
Year R**
© A & C Black 1999

Snap: picture cards

- **Cut out the cards.**

- **Count the animals in each picture.**

- **Match each picture card to a number card and a word card.**

| 3 | three |  |

Teachers' note Use the cards on this page with those on page 34. As a further extension, the children could play 'snap' or 'pairs' with two of the three sets of number, word and picture cards.

**Developing Numeracy
Numbers and the Number System
Year R
© A & C Black 1999**

All aboard!

- **Draw a line to match each anchor to a boat.**

five

ten

three

four

nine

two

six

seven

one

eight

 1

3

2

 7

9

8

6

4

5

10

 **Now try this!**

- **Draw people in each boat to match the number word.**

 three

Developing Numeracy
Numbers and the Number System
Year R
© A & C Black 1999

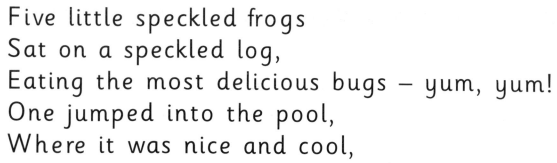

Five little speckled frogs

Five little speckled frogs
Sat on a speckled log,
Eating the most delicious bugs – yum, yum!
One jumped into the pool,
Where it was nice and cool,
    Then there were four
        speckled frogs.

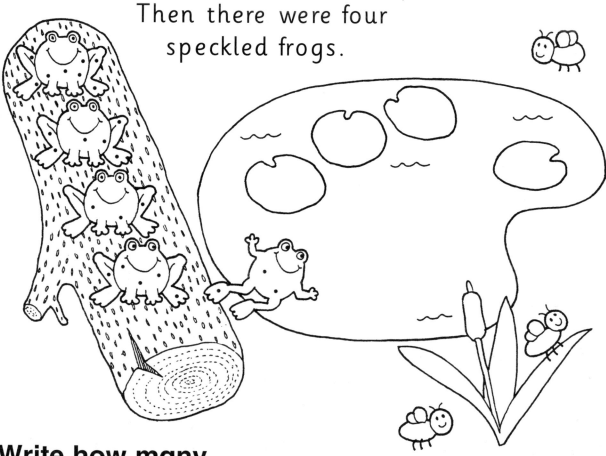

- **Write how many**

frogs [ ]   bugs [ ]   lilypads [ ]

- **Draw more bugs so there is one bug for each frog.**

- **Draw more lilypads so there is one lilypad for each frog.**

Teachers' note As a class, read or sing the rhyme with actions, with five children acting as the speckled frogs. Develop the activity by putting counters on the picture of the frogs as the rhyme is said or sung.

Developing Numeracy
Numbers and the Number System
Year R
© A & C Black 1999

Buzz, buzz, buzz

• **Count how many.**

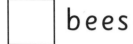 bees    flowers    beehives

• **Draw more flowers, bees and beehives to make**

3 flowers 5 bees 2 beehives

Teachers' note The children could use counters to help count the flowers, bees and hives, for example, take three counters, place two of them on the flowers – how many more flowers are needed?

Developing Numeracy
Numbers and the Number System
Year R
© A & C Black 1999

Jumping rabbit game

- **This is a game for 2 players.**
- **Take turns to roll a dice to move.**

start

finish

go on 2

go on 2

go on 3

go on 1

go on 4

go on 4

go on 5

go on 6

Teachers' note Photocopy this sheet on to A3 size paper or card. Each pair of children will need a copy of this page, a dice and two counters. Once the children are confident with the rules of the game, you could develop it by including 'penalty' squares, for example 'miss a turn', 'go back 4'.

**Developing Numeracy
Numbers and the Number System
Year R**
© A & C Black 1999

39

On the beach

- **Count the objects.**
- **Write the numbers in the boxes.**

| 1 | umbrella |

| | crabs | | starfish | | beach towels |

| | ice creams | | spades | | sandcastles |

- **How many of each type of shell can you count?**

Developing Numeracy
Numbers and the Number System
Year R
© A & C Black 1999

On the farm

- **Draw a different number of animals in each field.**
- **Write the numbers in the boxes.**

- **Which field has** most **animals in it?**
- **Which field has** least **animals in it?**

Teachers' note Ask for an oral response for the extension activity. Ask how the children know which field has most/least animals.

Developing Numeracy
Numbers and the Number System
Year R
© A & C Black 1999

Number fishing

• **Count how many**

children ☐

trees ☐

ducks ☐

1, 2, 3, 4, 5,
Once I caught a fish alive,
6, 7, 8, 9, 10,
Then I let it go again.

Now try this!

• **Draw 8 fish in the pond.**

• **Colour 5 fish red and 3 fish yellow.**

Developing Numeracy
Numbers and the Number System
Year R
© A & C Black 1999

At the party

- **Count how many cakes on each tray.**

- **Draw a line to match each tray to a number.**

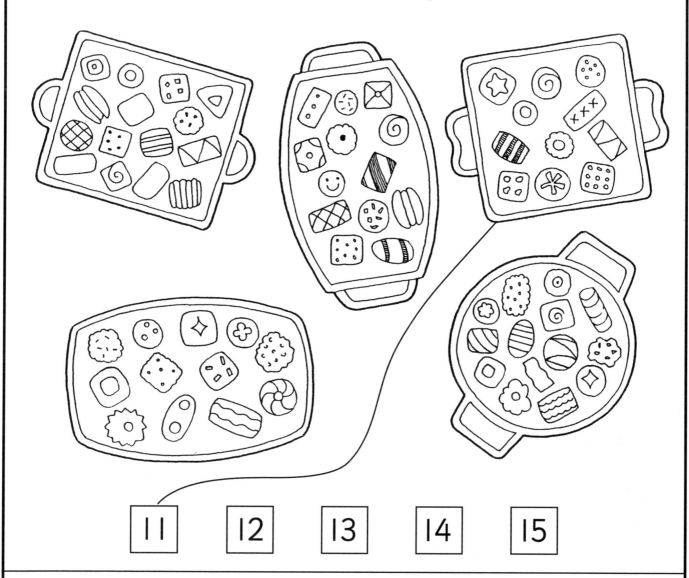

| 11 | 12 | 13 | 14 | 15 |

- **Draw more hats to make 15 party hats.**

Developing Numeracy
Numbers and the Number System
Year R
© A & C Black 1999

Paint pots

- **Draw some paint brushes in each pot.**

- **Write the numbers in the boxes.**

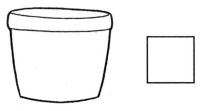

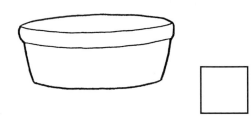

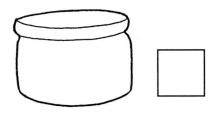

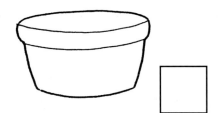

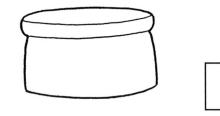

- **Which pot has the** most **brushes in it?**
- **Colour it blue.**
- **Which pot has the** least **brushes in it?**
- **Colour it yellow.**

Teachers' note Ask the children to draw a different number of brushes in each pot.

Developing Numeracy
Numbers and the Number System
Year R
© A & C Black 1999

• **Draw more balls to match the number in the box.**

| 4 | 3 | 5 |

| 7 | 6 |

• **Count the acrobats.**

• **Write the number in the box.**

Teachers' note The children could use counters to match the numbers in the boxes. This may help them work out how many more balls are needed for each juggler.

Developing Numeracy
Numbers and the Number System
Year R
© A & C Black 1999

Money banks

- **Draw some pennies in each money bank.**
- **Write the number in the box.**

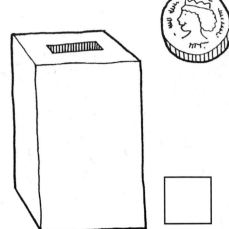

- **Colour red the bank with the** most **pennies.**
- **Colour blue the bank with the** fewest **pennies.**

Teachers' note Remind the children to draw a different number of pennies in each money bank.

**Developing Numeracy
Numbers and the Number System
Year R**
© A & C Black 1999

Little Red Riding Hood

- **This is a game for 2 players.**
- **Take turns to roll a dice to move.**

start

1

move on 2

2

move back 2

3

4

move back 1

5

6

move on 2

7

move back 4

8

9

10

11

move back 2

12

move on 1

13

move back 4

14

15

move on 2

16

move back 2

17

18

19

move back 1

20

finish

Grandma's Cottage

Teachers' note Photocopy this page on to A3 paper or card. Each pair of children will need a copy of this page, a dice and two counters. One child of the pair can be the wolf and the other Little Red Riding Hood!

Developing Numeracy
Numbers and the Number System
Year R
© A & C Black 1999

• **Continue the number pattern in each row.**

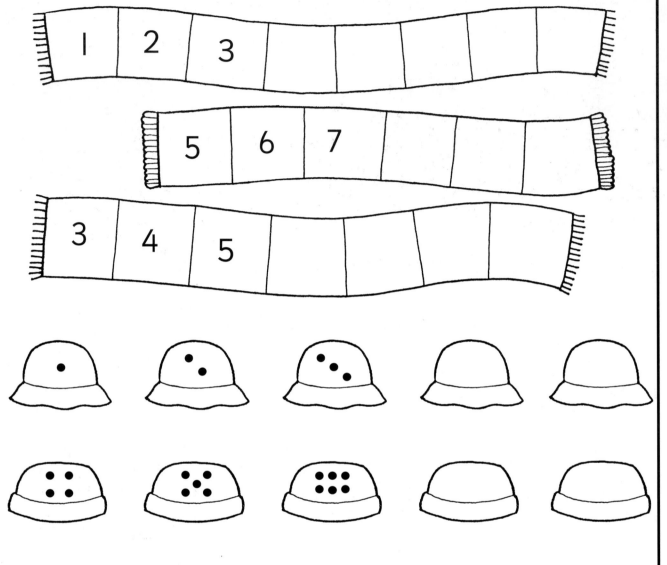

| 1 | 2 | 3 | | | | | |

| | 5 | 6 | 7 | | | |

| 3 | 4 | 5 | | | | |

• **Write your own number pattern.**

Teachers' note When the children have completed the sheet, they can work in pairs, covering a number in any of the patterns for a partner to work out.

Developing Numeracy
Numbers and the Number System
Year R
© A & C Black 1999

Counting patterns 2

• **Write the missing numbers in each row.**

• **Draw the missing spots in each row.**

• **Write your own number pattern.**

• **Write your own number pattern.**

Teachers' note When the children have completed the sheet, they can work in pairs, covering a number in any of the patterns for a partner to work out.

**Developing Numeracy
Numbers and the Number System
Year R**
© A & C Black 1999

Count backwards 1

• **Continue the number pattern in each row.**

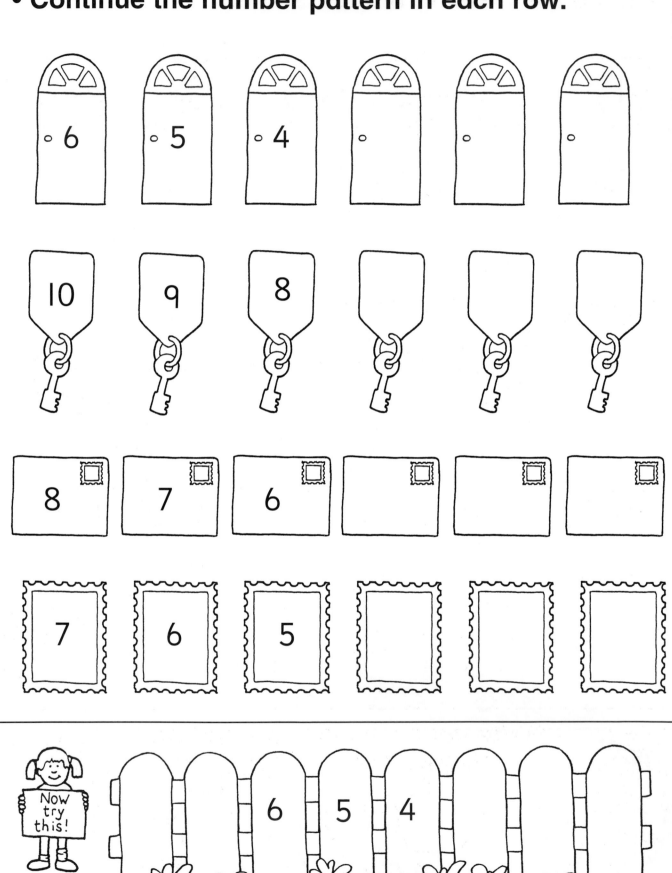

Teachers' note Look at each sequence with the children and ask them to predict the next number at each end of the sequence. Extend the activity by asking the children to colour the odd and even numbers. Some children may need a number line to help them with this activity.

Developing Numeracy
Numbers and the Number System
Year R
© A & C Black 1999

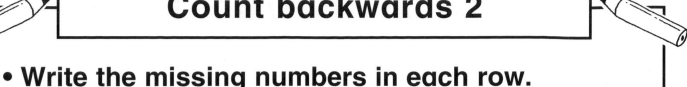

Count backwards 2

- **Write the missing numbers in each row.**

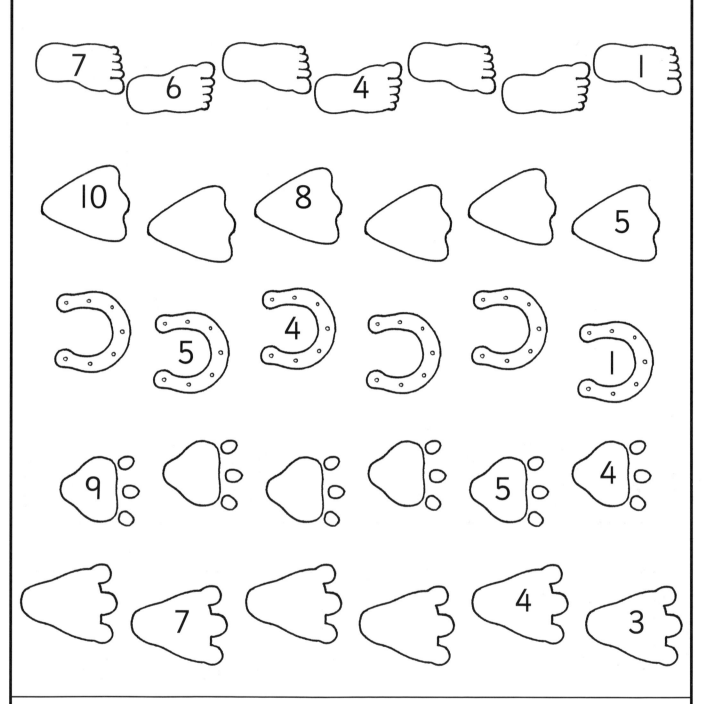

| 7 | 6 | | 4 | | | 1 |

| 10 | | 8 | | | 5 |

| | 5 | 4 | | | 1 |

| 9 | | | | 5 | 4 |

| | 7 | | | 4 | 3 |

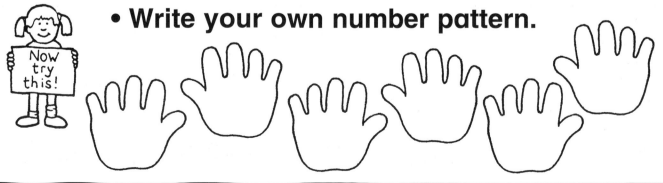

- **Write your own number pattern.**

Now try this!

Teachers' note Some children may need a number line to help them with this activity.

Developing Numeracy
Numbers and the Number System
Year R
© A & C Black 1999

51

Fruit salad

• **Continue the number pattern in each row.**

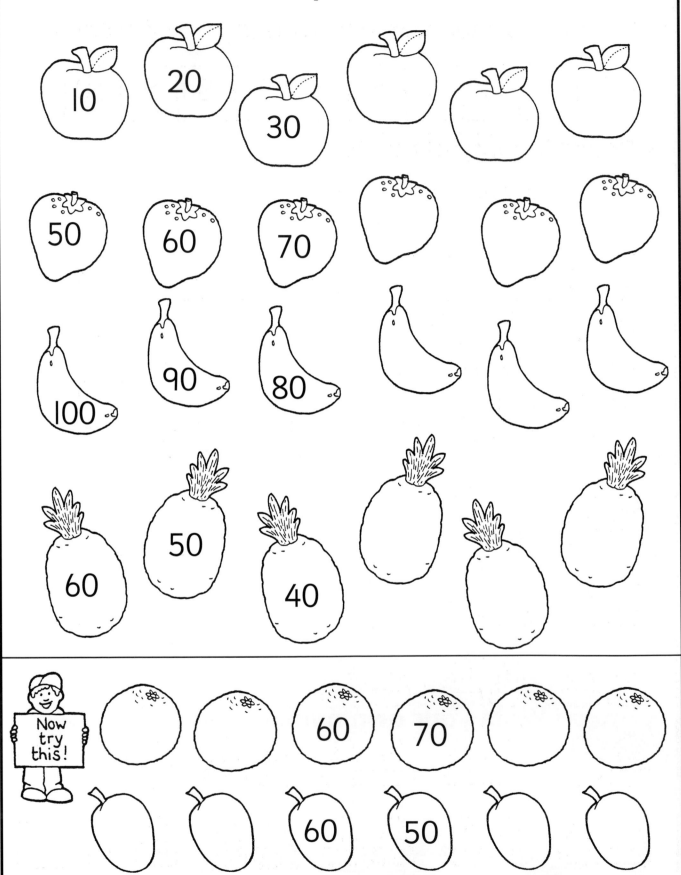

10 20 30

50 60 70

100 90 80

60 50 40

Now try this!

60 70

60 50

Teachers' note As a whole class introduction to this activity, use a blank number line (which you have marked in tens) to count in tens to 100. Have the number line available for children who are completing the sheet to look at for support.

Developing Numeracy
Numbers and the Number System
Year R
© A & C Black 1999

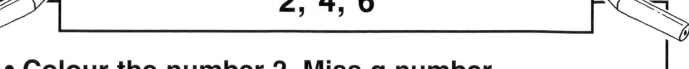

2, 4, 6

- **Colour the number 2. Miss a number.**

  Colour the next number. Continue to the end.

1	2	3	4	5	6	7	8	9	10

- **Count the objects in 2s.**

- **Write the number in the box.**

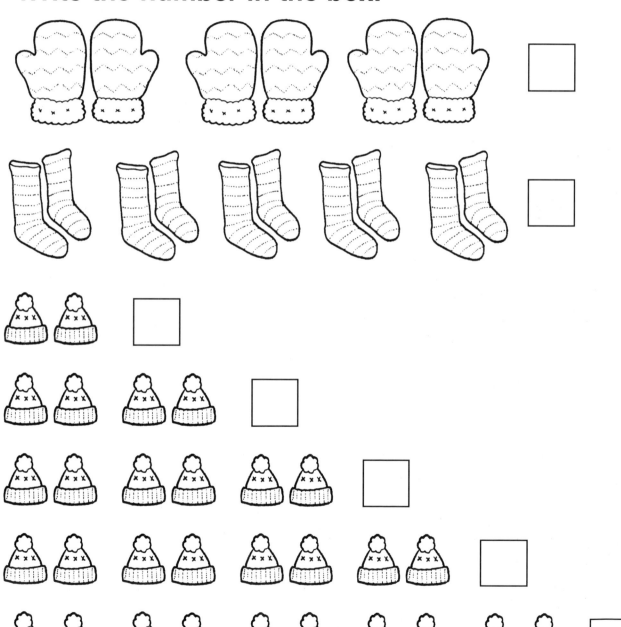

Developing Numeracy
Numbers and the Number System
Year R
© A & C Black 1999

Teachers' note When counting in twos as a class, whisper and shout alternate numbers to emphasise the pattern: 1, <u>2</u>, 3, <u>4</u>, 5, <u>6</u>.

Count in 2s

- ## Write how many cars. Count in 2s.

- ## Write how many planes. Count in 2s.

- ## Write how many   boats [ ]   buses [ ]

Now try this!

Teachers' note As a further extension activity, the children could count interlocking cubes in pairs, matching them to numbers on a number line. A group of children could also stand at the front of the class in pairs. Other children could be chosen to count them in twos.

Developing Numeracy
Numbers and the Number System
Year R
© A & C Black 1999

Motor race game

- **This is a game for 2 players.**
- **Roll a dice to move.**
- **Follow the instructions.**

start

count to ten

count back from ten

count in 2s to ten

count back from five

count to five

count from five to ten

count in 2s to eight

count to ten

count back from five

count from three to seven

finish

Teachers' note Photocopy this page on to A3 paper or card. Each pair of children will need a copy of this page, a dice and two counters. Children could be given additional instructions, for example, if they count correctly they move forward two squares. Children should count aloud.

**Developing Numeracy
Numbers and the Number System
Year R**
© A & C Black 1999

Spotty monsters

- **How many spots does this monster have?**

- **Colour blue the monsters with** `more` **spots.**

- **Colour yellow the monsters with** `fewer` **spots than this monster.**

Now try this!

Teachers' note Make sure the children realise that the extension activity refers back to the main illustration. Ask them which monster they have coloured blue and yellow. Then ask them which monster has one more, three more or six more spots than the monster at the top. The activity provides an opportunity to use language such as 'greater than', 'smaller amounts' and so on.

**Developing Numeracy
Numbers and the Number System
Year R**
© A & C Black 1999

How much is it?

- **Draw 10 pieces of food.**
- **Cut out the price labels.**
- **Give each piece of food a price label.**
- **Put them in order.**

Start with the lowest price.

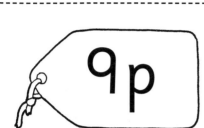

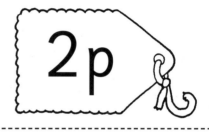

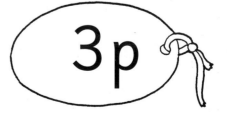

Teachers' note Children could draw the pieces of food on ten squares of paper which could then be stuck on a large piece of paper in ascending price order. The activity provides an opportunity for the children to develop their knowledge of mathematical vocabulary, such as 'more than', 'less than' and 'greater/smaller amounts'.

**Developing Numeracy
Numbers and the Number System
Year R**
© A & C Black 1999

Number trains

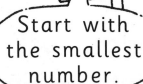

- **Cut out the carriages and the trains.**
- **Stick the carriages on the trains in order.**

Start with the smallest number.

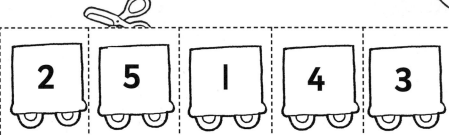

| 2 | 5 | 1 | 4 | 3 |

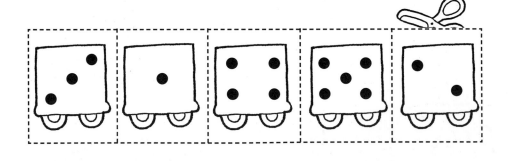

Teachers' note Photocopy this page on to A3 paper. This activity provides an opportunity to use the language of comparison with the children, for example: 'Which number is more than three and less than five? Which numbers are smaller than five? Which number is greater, four or five?'

**Developing Numeracy
Numbers and the Number System
Year R**
© A & C Black 1999

Snakes and ladders

• **Write the missing numbers on the snakes and ladders.**

Numbers visible on the snakes and ladders:

Top snake: 2, 3, 4

Left ladder: 7, 6, 5

Middle snake: 4, 5, 6

Right ladder: 5, 4, 3

Bottom ladder: 2, 1

Bottom snake: 2, 3

Teachers' note As an extension activity, ask the children to colour the even numbers on the snakes and the odd numbers on the ladders, counting in twos.

Developing Numeracy
Numbers and the Number System
Year R
© A & C Black 1999

Number beads

- **Join the beads together in order.**

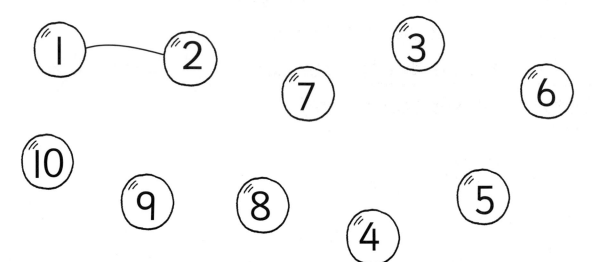

- **Add your own numbers to each set of beads.**

- **Join the beads together in order.**

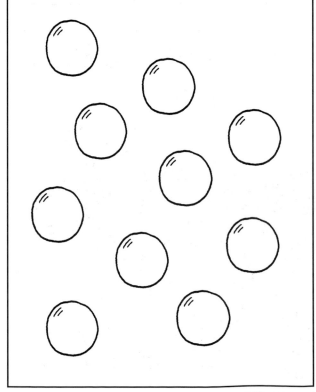

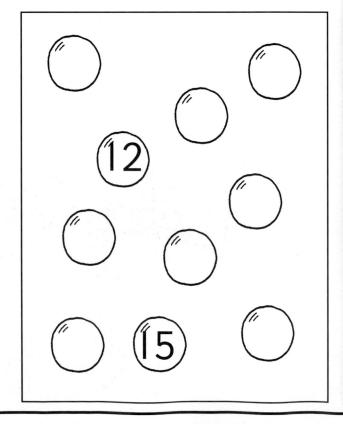

Teachers' note In the extension activity, encourage the children to use the numbers between ten and twenty (or beyond). They should write sequential numbers on the beads so that they can join them in order, for example 12, 13, 14, 15; not 12, 15, 17.

**Developing Numeracy
Numbers and the Number System
Year R**
© A & C Black 1999

All in order

- Colour the 1st person blue.
- Draw a bag for the 2nd person.
- Colour the 3rd person green.
- Draw a hat on the 4th person.
- Colour the 5th person red.

| 1st | 2nd | 3rd | 4th | 5th |

- Write the order on the rosettes to show where each horse will finish.

Now try this!

Teachers' note Read the labels 1st-5th with the children and explain that these are short for 'first', 'second', 'third' and so on.

Developing Numeracy
Numbers and the Number System
Year R
© A & C Black 1999

61

• **Cut out the cards.**

0	1
2	3
4	5
6	7
8	9

Teachers' note Cut out the cards and use them for 'show me' activities (see introduction pages 5 and 6).

Developing Numeracy
Numbers and the Number System
Year R
© A & C Black 1999

Numeral cards 1 to 20

• **Cut out the cards.**

1	2	3	4
5	6	7	8
9	10	11	12
13	14	15	16
17	18	19	20

Teachers' note Cut out the cards and use them for 'show me' activities (see introduction pages 5 and 6).

**Developing Numeracy
Numbers and the Number System
Year R**
© A & C Black 1999

I can count to 10

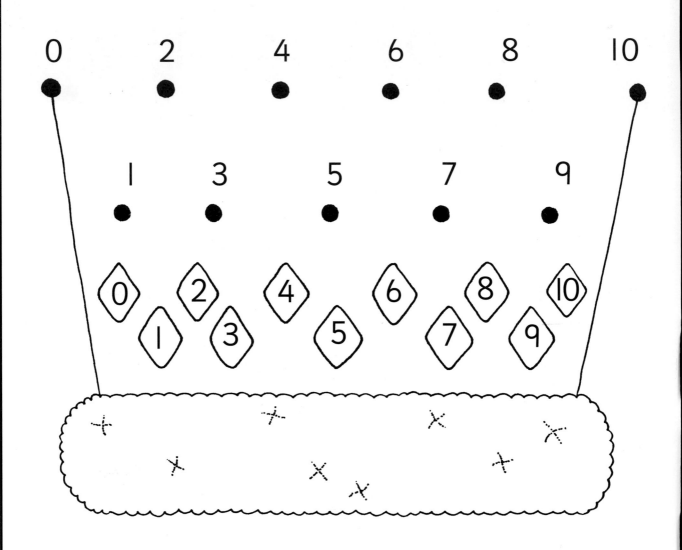

Well done!

(Write your name here)

Teachers' note Encourage the children to join the dots to complete the picture (they could count aloud as they do so), then to colour it in.

**Developing Numeracy
Numbers and the Number Syste
Year R**
© A & C Black 1999